MAKING UP WITH JB

This paperback edition first published in 2018
by Delere Press LLP

Block 370G Alexandra Road
#09-09 Singapore 159960
www.delerepress.com
Delere Press LLP reg no. T11LL1061K

Designed by Sarah and Schooling

© text by Jeremy Fernando, 2018
© photographs by John WP Phillips, 2018
© epilogue by Marine Dupuis Baudrillard, 2018

All Rights Reserved

MAKING UP WITH JB

followed by

A FINAL PARADOXIAL WINK...

by Jeremy Fernando

alongside photographs by John WP Phillips
with an epilogue by Marine Dupuis Baudrillard

Delere Press

Contents

Making up with JB 1
A Final Paradoxical Wink... 33
Un Épilogue 43
Contributors 47

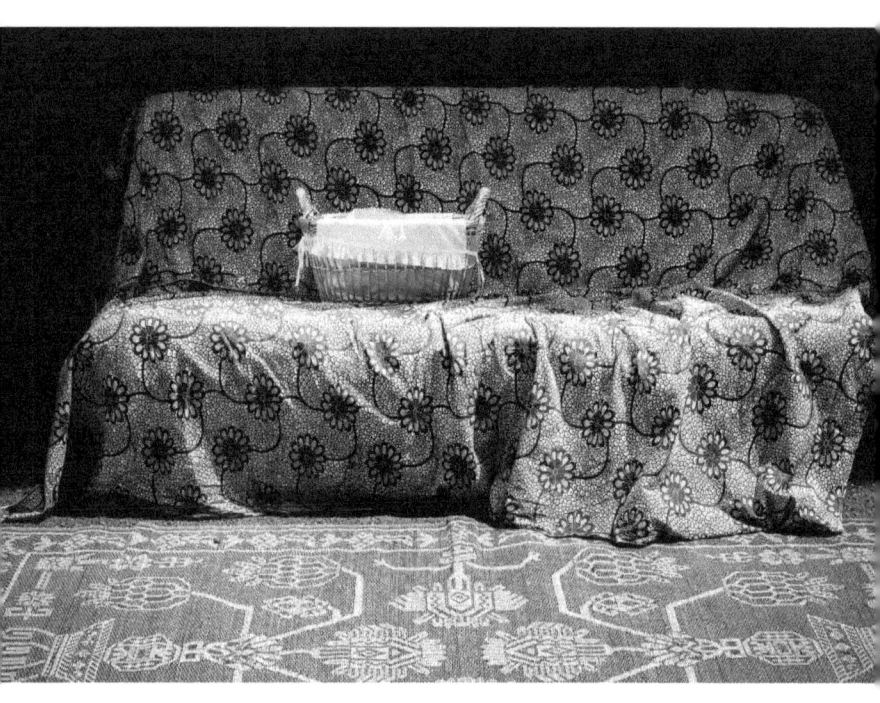

As I do not know how to start, I shall say that my name is Jeremy Fernando *and that I am* the Jean Baudrillard Fellow at The European Graduate School *and that now I feel a deep sense of relief because I can move on to the second sentence, which is always less compromising than the first, which is always the most important in any text, since in the first, as is well known, the greatest care is never enough.*[i]

For, the first, the origin—the *auctor*—is always mysterious, unknown, unknowable: where despite all possible care, one can never quite know what one is attending to. After all, how can one even begin to attend to a void?

Which is the question that has been haunting me, that I suspect will always be haunting me, at least since the 6th of March 2017— a haunting that might have waited ten years, has quite possibly been awaiting me for a decade.

The question of: *what does one do after one has made JB disappear.* Not helped to—nothing so vain; for, it is not as if JB ever needed any help in that respect—but made. Crafted. Brought forth.

---

[i] « As I do not know how to start, I shall say that my name is Marcel Maniere and that I belong to the OuLiPo and that now I feel a deep sense of relief because I can move on to the second sentence, which is always less compromising than the first, which is always the most important in any book, since in the first, as is well known, the greatest care is never enough ».

Enrique Vila-Matas. *Bartleby & Co.*, translated by Jonathan Dunne. London: Vintage, 2004: 140.

Perhaps let's temper that a little: *made* seems to be an overstatement, though its echoes will remain with us throughout this—chapter, piece, sound, echo, of my attempt to respond to, continue after, my attempt to continue responding after, the text called, the book named, entitled even, *Why hasn't JB already disappeared*.[ii] All whilst sending apologies, culpabilities, my *mea culpa*, to not just JB, but to all of the other people who were involved in the text, in the book that was my attempt to respond to the ghosts of a text message from a decade ago; a missive sent by my dear friend, Tombie Rautenbach, that arrived at three in the morning on 7 March 2007—a text which read, « Baudrillard is dead ».

Perhaps what also haunts me is the fact that *Why hasn't JB already disappeared* is not in the form of a question—it is a somewhat statement: through a statement containing a question in it. So, perhaps always also a quest; one in which I cannot quite deny—at least not convincingly—that there might have been a longing for his disappearance. After all, as Nietzsche has long taught us, *it is the ones who calls themselves your fellow that you should beware, whom you should be aware of.*

For, what might it mean to call oneself a fellow, to call myself a fellow of JB?
To claim to be with, to stake a claim of being with, perhaps even to even lie down with (**legh*), to stand beside—to declare a certain loyalty, even a fidelity, towards. But, at the same time, the notion of fellowship is always also haunted by the echo of membership, of a price of entry, always resounds with echoes of a *fee*: both in terms of something that one has to leave at the door in order to enter, and perhaps also a certain remuneration that one gains from being a part of, perhaps even something that one is paid to be part of.

[ii] *Why hasn't JB already disappeared* is an attempt to respond to a text message, a textual call—to a missive sent by Tombie Rautenbach that arrived at three in the morning on 7 March 2007—which read, « Baudrillard is dead ». But more than a eulogy, more than a mourning—if such a thing is possible—this is an attempt to think with Baudrillard, all whilst keeping in mind the fact that his work, his writing, his thought, always brings with it a little chuckle, a sly grin.

So, perhaps an attempt at the impossible: thinking with a smile at a point where there might not have been much, if anything, to smile about.

Trying never to forget that in attempting to speak with the dead, one always also runs the risk of rewriting them, writing over them, quite possibly effacing them. But, of course, Baudrillard already knew this: after all, he was the one who called for his own disappearance even before his death.

So perhaps, this book is an imaginative response: a reading in fidelity to JB; not to the man—nothing so banal—nor even to his work; but a reading that opens itself to the possibility of the grin of the one who has already disappeared, to the shadow of his silent smile.

The responses are composed of writings by Jeremy Fernando; alongside translations by Setsuko Adachi & Daniel Kwang Guan Chan; a poem by Laura Parker; art-works by Russell Bennetts, Cecília Erismann, Michael Kearney, Sorelle Henricus, Julia Hölzl, Grace Euna Kim, Jeanette Lamb, John WP Phillips, Kenny Png, Kristy Trinier, Sean Smith, and Berit Jane Soli-Holt.

These conversations between—perhaps even attempted séances by—the various texts, modes of responses, were mediated by Yanyun Chen.

Jeremy Fernando. *Why hasn't JB already disappeared*. Singapore: Delere Press, 2017.

Which means: it is to add another onto oneself, at the very same time as one is adding oneself onto another.

Just like make up.
In which one is never quite sure whether something is being added onto one, or if one is bringing forth—highlighting—some feature, some aspect, that is always already within one. After all, one can apply *nude* make-up; where what is added on is more or less exactly the same colour, is meant to be exactly the same colour, as what is under; where what is highlighted and what is covered-up is precisely the same tinge, the same thing. Where *before* and *after* is—as our Thai friends so eloquently put it—*same same but different*.

Here, one can be cynical and claim that *same same but different* is a mere sales pitch, an attempt to charge more for the same thing—where it is nothing but a performative claim of difference. After all, one hears this phrase mostly from shopkeepers who have been accused of charging more than another vender for the same item. However, if one does so, one would be missing the possibility of attending to another reading: that one can only make a claim about something in a specific situation; that the same thing in another context is also different—that all claims are singular. Which opens the dossier that an object is never just an object: if one is attempting to attend to it, one has to respond to it in its throwness into the world. Even more pertinently, *same same but different* opens the possibility that difference(s) can lie beyond our cognition, be outside of, exterior to, our knowledge; that what we know is bound by our phenomenological finitude. That—as Plato has taught us—to truly know we have to be inspired, struck from elsewhere. But since the divine is always already beyond us, there is no way of knowing if we are inspired or not, if we are hearing

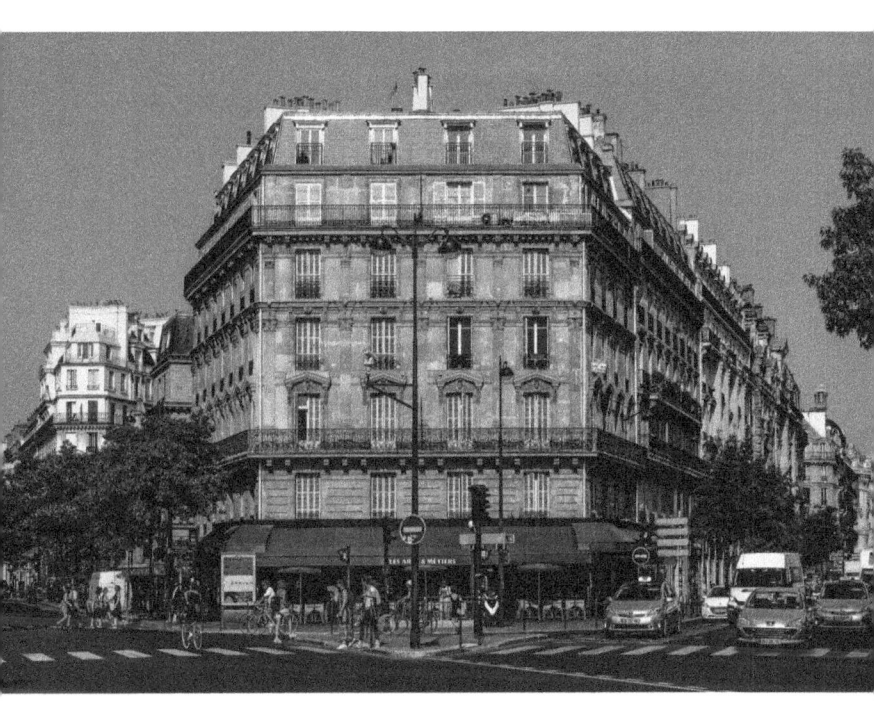

the whispers of the *daemon* or merely voices in our head; if our repetition is really any *different*, or just *same same*.

And whenever we hear the phrase, we might also try not to forget that *same* appears twice, as a pair, in tandem, as a duo. Thus, we should perhaps consider the possibility that the duality, the doubling of the *same*, draws our attention to the fact that something can only be different when there is something else to be different from. Which is not to say that difference itself, difference only, relies on another; however, without an other (even if this other is itself, is oneself, at another moment, situation, context) there cannot be any difference. Hence, even as every statement relies on relationality—on a correspondence, imagined or otherwise, between what is said and something, or some relation, in the world—this very relationality also foregrounds difference; this relationality also reminds us that *same* is like *same* but is not necessarily the *same;* a duality that continues dueling whilst never ceasing, cutting, enacting a *caesura* on being a duo.

Thus, *same-ness* and *difference* are not necessarily antonyms, but always already rely on each other, are potentially part of each other.

So, even as one might say that cosmetics are a form of camouflage, that they help one to hide something, to hide away even, blend into the surroundings, one should try not to forget that the echo of *cosmos* is never quite so far behind each application. For, *cosmetics*, the highest form of artifice, re-appearance has always been a question of *beauty*, of *truth*.

Which is not to say that we are necessarily in the arena of truth—nothing so banal—but that each time there is make-up, we might well be playing with not just the notion of *beauty*, but always also a wholeness that lies in what cannot be known, perhaps cannot even be seen.

Where what one might well be doing is dabbling in *l'empire de l'ombre*, in the realm of the shadows.

Which is quite possibly the lesson of the allegory of the cave: that it is not so much that we should be looking out of the cave—for, staring at the sun only leads to more blindness, to complete blindness even—but that one should make better shadows. Which might well be why Socrates or Plato—the two quite possibly remaining indistinguishable, shadows of each other—were suspicious of artists, of art itself: for, what else is artifice but the making of beautiful shadows.

And if art is about transformation, movement—perhaps even a shift in form from *tekhnē*, from craft, into something else brought about by the whispers of a *daemon*—it is no wonder that Slavoj Žižek claims that « art lies in the gap between the frame and the viewer ».

For, art is nothing other than	*You reached for the secret too soon*
a praise of *shadows*,	*You cried for the moon*
éloge de l'ombre.	*Shine on you crazy diamond.*

— David Gilmour, Roger Waters, Richard Wright

Which opens—or perhaps leaves us with—the question: exactly what shadows are we making here, or attending to. For, all we have left of our friend JB are his words, the texts he leaves with us; and all I have to attend to them, to write on them, to speak to them, are words. And even as words abandon us, as Sam Beckett might say, at the same time, « it's only words, and words

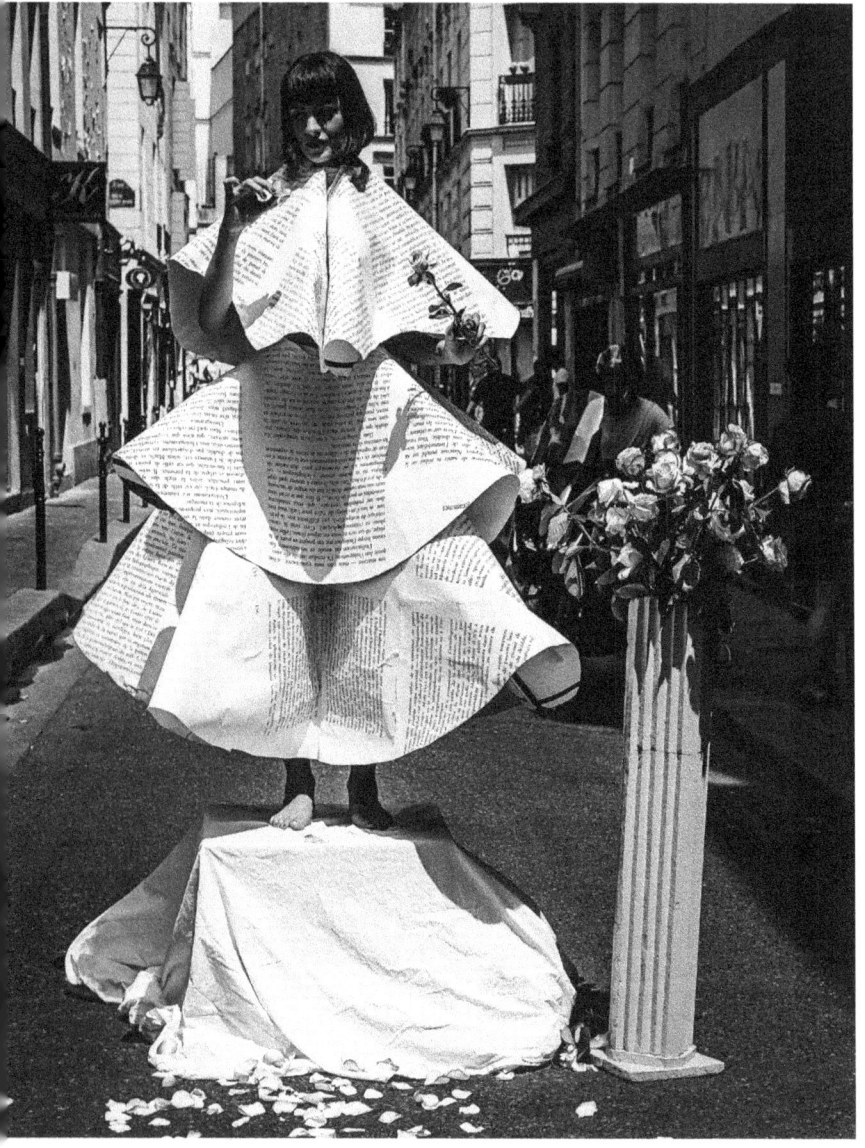

are all I have, to take your heart away »[iii]. But, it is perhaps in their abandonment, in their abandoning us, in leaving us to wait—keeping in mind the teachings of both Sam and Maurice Blanchot; that *waiting* is the very limit and condition of thought itself—in abandoning us to wait, that words open the space for the possibility of something to come, for the very potentiality of an event.

Even if that event is death itself.

Which is why it's much too easy to say—and, at the same time, much too difficult, perhaps even impossible to—*forget Baudrillard*. So I shall leave that one to Sylvère, to my dear teacher, Sylvère Lotringer.

And continue to attempt to attend to JB's words, his thoughts—continue to echo him in my words, my thoughts.

And here, it is not too difficult to hear an echo of the teachings of another dear teacher of mine, echoes of Werner Hamacher, when he says, « echo, citation, mirrors are no harmless utensils of the beautification of an appearance. They are the instruments of an evacuation, a dispossession, and a making infinite of what was said in the mere saying »[iv].

At any rate, removing meaning brings out the essential point: namely, that the image is more important than what it speaks about — just as language is more important than what it signifies.

But it must also remain alien to itself in some way. Not reflect (on) itself as a medium, not take itself for an image. It must remain a fiction, a fable and hence echo the irresolvable fiction of the event.

— Jean Baudrillard

Of both reminding us that JB is no longer here—even when he was here with us, each time we marshaled his voice, summoned his words for us, we were appropriating him, recontextualising him, decontextualising him, taking him, apprehending him, for our own—and always also with us as we hear, every time we attempt to listen to, his words, his voice. For, even as speaking of him, writing on him, might well be a writing on, speaking over, writing out, JB, we should try not to forget Hélène Cixous' beautiful reminder that « citation is the voice of the other and it highlights the double playing of the narrative authority. We constantly hear the footsteps of the other, the footsteps of others in language, others speaking in Stephen's language or in Ulysses', I mean in the book's language... It reminds us that we have been caught up in citation ever since we said the first words mama or papa »[v].

Which perhaps allows us to return to one of our first questions: that of *how one can even begin to attend to a void?* Perhaps only through citation, by attending to the voice of another—not just of mama or papa, but precisely in calling on them, in calling them as such.

[iii] Barry Gibb, Robin Gibb, & Maurice Gibb. Words. London: Polydor Records, 1967.

[iv] Werner Hamacher, 'For—Philology' in *Minima Philologica*, translated by Catharine Diehl & Jason

[v] Hélène Cixous. *Stigmata.* London: Routledge, 2005: 135.

That each time we cite JB, refer to him, turn to him, we are not just resurrecting him—at least, a version of him—we might well also be calling him *daddy*. So, not so much that the author is dead, but that each time we read him, we are writing the author—authoring the authority of the *auctor*—into being. Foregrounding the fact—reminding us, if you prefer—that in reading what is also being written is the very notion of the author; which may or may not have anything to do with the one who writes, the one who has written, almost certainly nothing to do with the one doing the writing.

Out of honest respect for true authorship, I quote the world, I quoted it, since it was neither me nor mine.

— Clarice Lispector

And that all of this takes place in that space, that void—which is precisely the space of waiting that allows us to read, which allows for the possibility of reading to take place. Which means, somewhat ironically, that even in reading, the very thing we cannot be sure of is whether we are reading something, attending to the text, or writing its very authoring into being—a writing that cannot take place without that very reading itself. Which also means that this is a reading that cannot be conceptualised as, that cannot be stabilised as a concept called, reading. Though, as Harold Bloom tries to never let us forget, « strip irony from reading, and it loses at once all discipline and all surprise… irony will clear your mind of the cant of the ideologues… To read… you must be able to read humanly, with all of you. You are more than an ideology, whatever your convictions »[vi]. Thus *reading*—recalling, re-reading, Werner's lesson to me over lunch one afternoon in Saas Fee—reading here is understood as the relation to an other that occurs prior to any semantic or formal identification, and therefore prior to any attempt at assimilating what is being read to the one who reads. As neither an act nor a rule-governed operation, *reading* needs to be thought as an event of an encounter with an other—and more precisely an other which is not the other as identified by the reader, but heterogeneous in relation to any identifying determination. Thus, a *pre-relational relationality* where what the reader encounters may only be encountered before any phenomenon; hence a non-phenomenal event or even the event of the undoing of all phenomenality.

Where irony is nothing other than another name for the space—the gap—needed for the possibility of reading. Keeping in mind Jean-Luc Nancy's beautiful reminder, that « it is space that is first needed to touch »[vi]. In other words—and here, there is perhaps nothing more apt than, we have possibly no choice other than to be, echoing the words of the other—reading is nothing other than opening oneself to the possibility of being touched by another.

And even if, even when, touched, the other quite possibly remains unknown to, hidden from, one.

And here, we should also try not to forget that it is impossible to choose to forget: that it happens to one, and that there is no object, nor referent, to forgetting. Thus, each act of memory, every

---

[vi] Harold Bloom. *How to Read and Why.* New York: Simon & Schuster, 2000: 27-28.

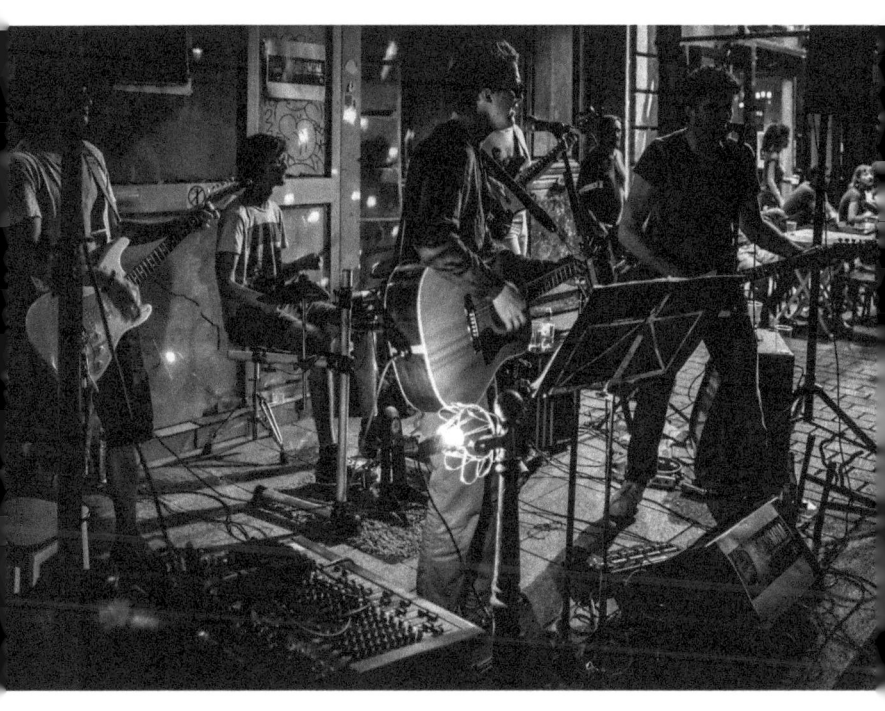

attempt at remembering, might well bring with it forgetting,
quite possibly has forgetting written into it. Which might well
be why Sylvère and JB could only attempt to *forget Baudrillard* in
and through a conversation: *un entretien infini*, as it were; for, the
forgetting might, and could possibly, only happen in the parts of
the dance, the turning around with each other, that remain silent,
or in the parts to come—the two remaining indistinguishable, in
a twist, perhaps in a *satantango* with each other.

In a continual quest with each other: keeping in mind that
the question is precisely the very characteristic, condition, of
intelligence itself—even as it remains its very limit; for, what is
evil in intelligence, what is *l'intelligence du mal*, is precisely the
fact that it is unable to prevent itself from questioning itself,
questioning itself as question. Where its status as question is itself
called into question, is precisely what is in question.

Which might well be why JB teaches us that « intelligence
cannot—and will never be able to—be in power: because it
consists precisely in this twofold refusal »[viii] : where it would rather
not be dominated, nor dominate.

[viii] Jean-Luc uttered this phrase in a seminar—entitled *Art, Community, &
Freedom*—at The European Graduate School in June 2006. At least that's how it
appears in my notes, my notations, of the seminar: so, there is a possibility that
it might only have been me hearing it; there is also the possibility that I might
have mis-heard, have taken down something that only I heard, that might never
have been said. I would, though, like to believe that in noting down, I was
responding to not only the cadences in Jean-Luc's voice, but the musicality in
his thinking, in his thought itself.

A refusal that is not quite a *no*: but a *not* that is always also *an affirmation* at exactly the same time—that keeps just enough power in order to *rather not*; that says *yes* to itself without necessarily knowing what exactly this self that it is, is.

A self that is an *I* in the same way that Werner Herzog might say *I* when he says: « I am fascinated by the possibilities for a deeper stratum of truth, although please don't ask me what I mean by truth, because nobody can answer that one. But, you see, we are creators. What I do is elevate the audience. I'm intensifying facts to such a degree that they start to get the glow of illumination for you. They acquire insight and poetry of an ecstatic nature, like medieval monks... I'm not interested in myself. You should not expose the deepest recesses of your own soul. It doesn't do anyone any good »[ix].

An *I* that can only speak from the position of the *I* whilst not-saying anything about the *I* : that lets the *I* die to itself as it speaks of *I*.

Or, as dearest Anne, Anne Dufourmantelle, might say: « to die so that a truth of the questioning of meaning may survive, and not to give that act the arrogance of a response, is to render to night its reality; the opposite of an abdication »[x].

[ix] Erik Hedegaard. 'Werner Herzog: The Art of Being a Death-Defying, Gonzo Filmmaking Genius' in *Rolling Stone*, March 2017.

[x] Jacques Derrida & Anne Dufourmantelle. *Of hospitality: Anne Dufourmantelle invites Jacques Derrida to respond*, translated by Rachel Bowlby. Stanford: Stanford University Press, 2000: 48.

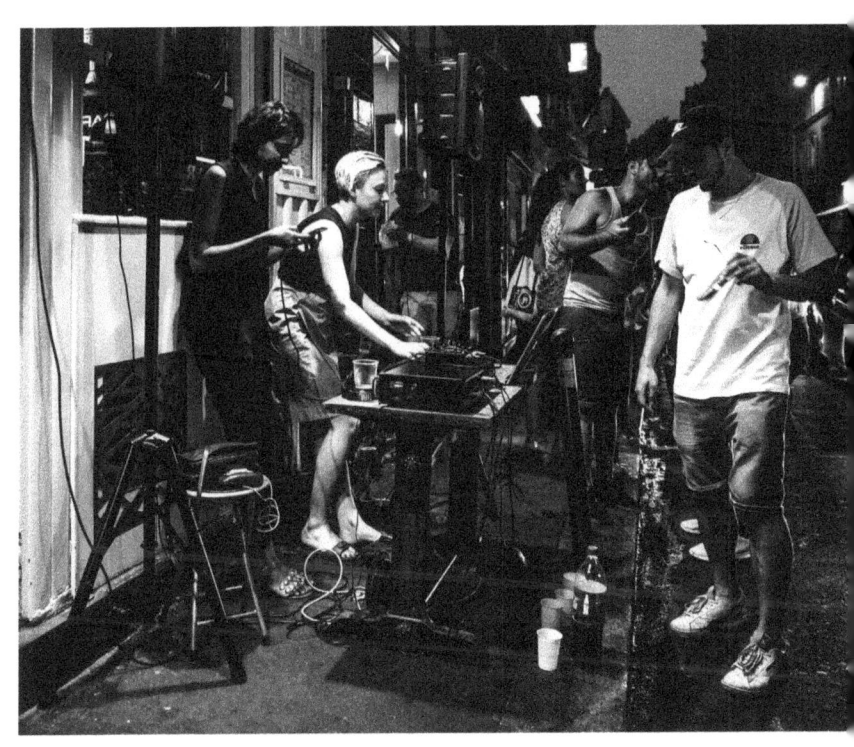

For, it is not as if any possible response to a truth—whatever that may mean—will come, can come, from us: through us perhaps, but almost certainly—though who is to say, so I will say—not from one. As JB once said, « *il y a une forme originale de répétition, celle qui traduit le fait qu'on n'a jamais qu'une seule idée dans sa vie (quand on a la chance d'en avoir une* »[xi]; that, there is an original form of repetition, the form that expresses the fact that *we never only have one idea in our lives (when we are even lucky enough to have one)*: that any idea that one has, not only comes to us but is always also an idea that is *same same but different*, that perhaps each time we see it as an idea, call it an idea, we have both recognised it, remembered it, as an idea, but at the same time have already forgotten all the other possibilities, all the other ideas, in, within, that come with, that said idea.

For, who would ever—I could never—know where the idea to write, to put together, *Why hasn't JB already disappeared*, came from: which is by no means a way of avoiding responsibility—for, regardless of the origin of the call, regardless of where the call emanated from, it was I who picked it up, picked up the phone, as it were. Even if one can never— I will never—know if it were only *voices in me head*.

If I were only making it all up.

[xi] Jean Baudrillard. 'Le Mal Ventriloque' dans *Carnival et cannibale*. Paris: Éditions de L'Herne, 2008: 36.

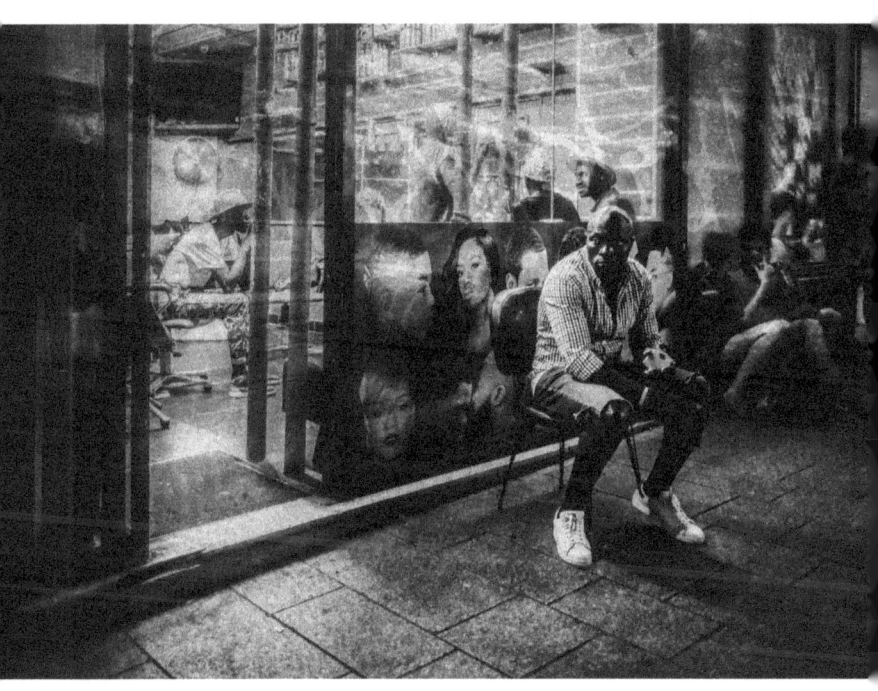

§

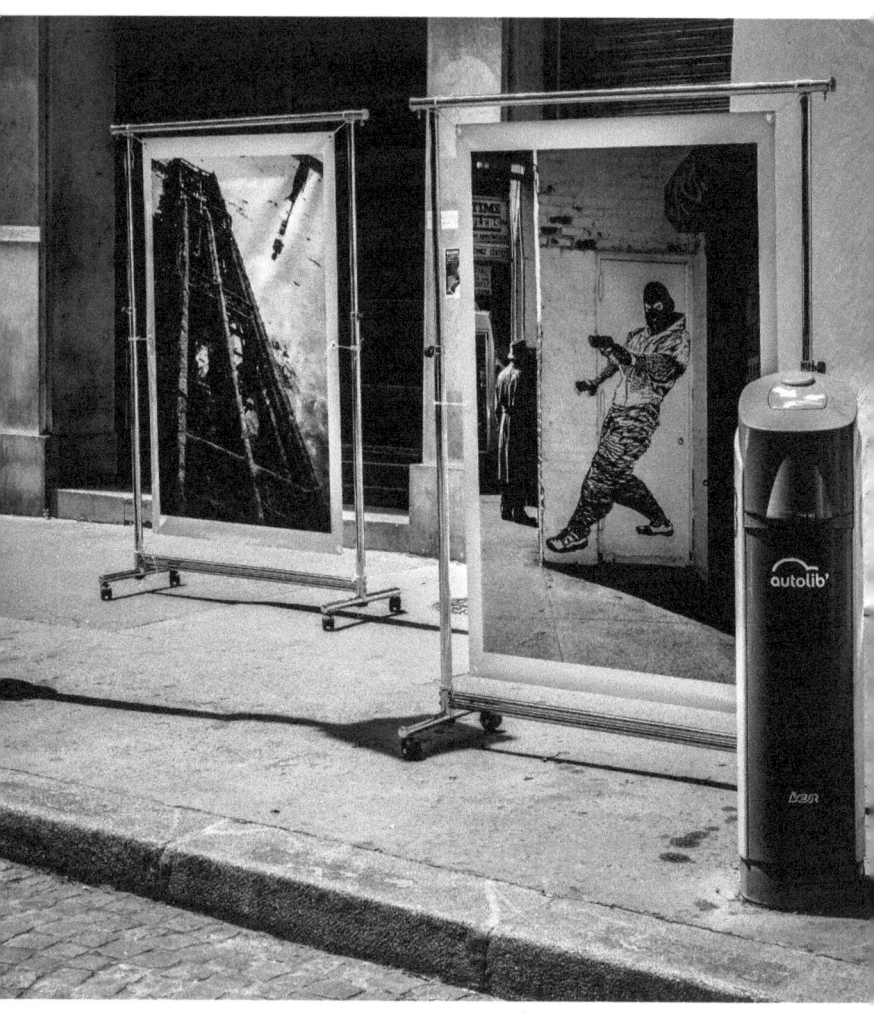

For, I am writing this on a warm afternoon in Singapore—let's imagine I'm writing this all at one go (it is so much prettier that way)—to be read out to you, maybe even by you, in this room. That what you are hearing, perhaps even listening to (why not indulge myself here), mayhaps even reading, has been written solely for you, *assigned only to you*. And that you, at some point, might ask me, or ask yourself, where all this is coming from, or headed to. And I would say, answer, respond—just so that you do not think you have failed to do anything—that *I would tell you if I knew*, and that there is perhaps one day when I might know, *just not yet*.

All not very likely, of course.
But as Johnny Marr—for, I'm not particularly fond of Morrissey—might sing, « for once in my life, let me get what I want. Lord knows it would be the first time »[xii].

Where perhaps *what I want* is for a fulfillment of a particular wish, regardless of how ironic it might have been when it was first uttered. The wish being: *that JB has disappeared*. For, as he has long taught us, « disappearing should be an art form, a seductive way of leaving the world. I believe that part of disappearing is to disappear before you die, to disappear before you have run dry, while you still have something to say »[xiii].

[xii] Johnny Marr & Morrissey. 'Please, Please, Please, Let Me Get What I Want', B-Side to *William, It Was Really Nothing*. London: Rough Trade Records, 1984.

[xiii] This quip comes from an unpublished interview in Oslo, and can also be found here:
http://www.eurozine.com/the-art-of-disappearing/

And perhaps, by continuing to ventriloquise, by continually ventriloquising, JB—through the artifice of bringing forth a voice, regardless of whether it is his or not, whether he might have wanted it or not—we have given him nothing other than the very space to disappear, a space in which to disappear.

For, we should bear in mind JB's reminder—in 'Le mal ventriloque', no less—that « there is a whole art in unfurling a body of thought in such a way that one ends up passing it by without seeing it. This is the opposite of discourse, which lays out its findings and arguments and sentences itself to house arrest within the precincts of its own conclusions »[xiv].

Where the art lies in not making the obvious obvious, but through the very reverse, in its very reversibility: in maintaining the secret in thought, in thinking, even whilst laying everything out, in laying bare—in keeping the secrecy that is nudity even while seemingly making everything naked.

And here, we should keep in mind the fact that secrets never lie in their content: that it is the recognition that they are secrets—of their form *as secret*—which is crucial. This can be seen in group secrets: for, since the entire group knows what the secret is, clearly the content of the secret is not as important as the fact that only members within the group are privy to this as secret. Occasionally, the actual content can be so trivial that even people outside the group know the information; they just do not realise, recognise, its significance. For instance, if I used my date of birth as the password to my bank account, merely knowing when I

[xiv] Jean Baudrillard. 'Ventriloquous Evil' in *Carnival and Cannibal*, translated by Chris Turner. London: Seagull Books, 2010: 34.

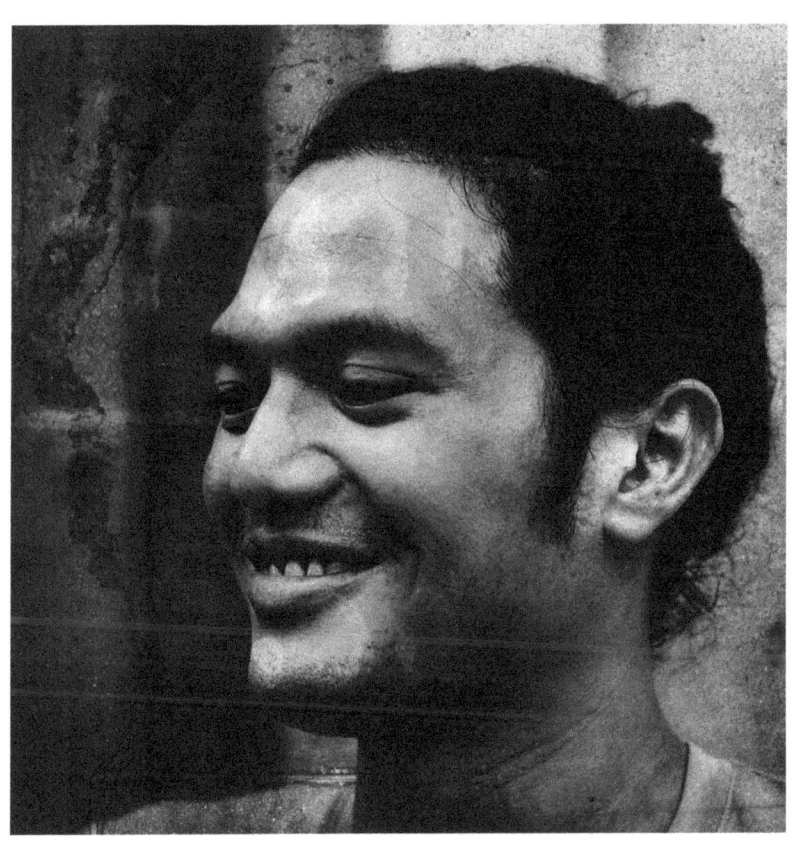

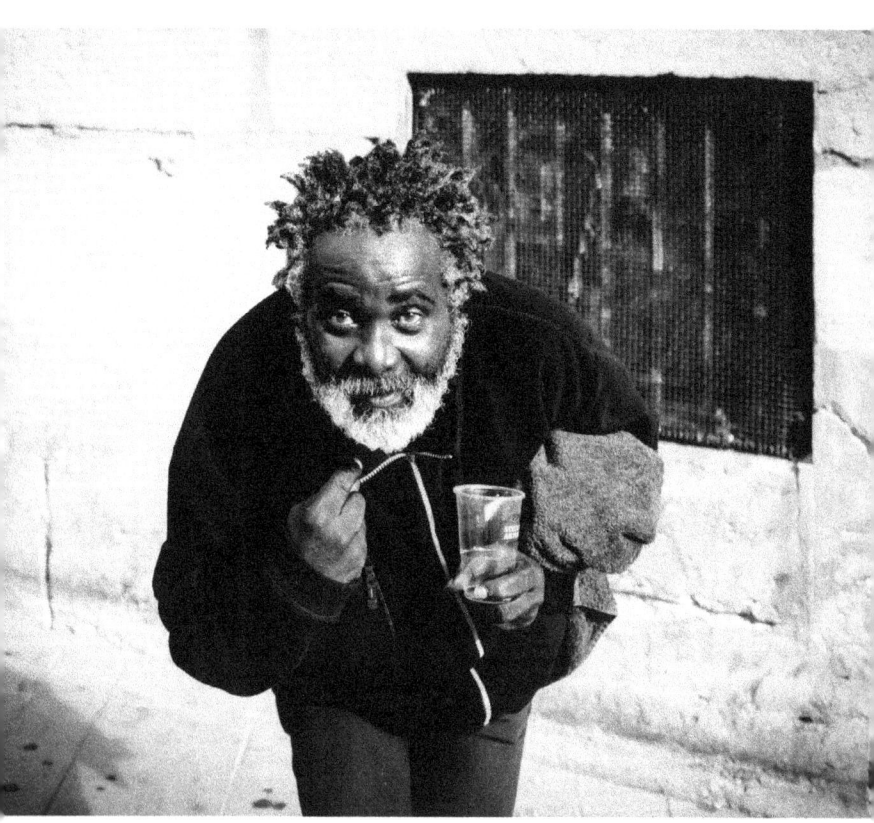

was born would not instantly give you the key to my life savings. In order for that to happen, one would have had to recognise the significance of the knowledge of my birthday. This means that one has to know that one knows something, has to know it *as* something—as secret. However, the moment one knows that something *is secret*, what is *secret about the secret* dissolves, disappears, is no longer secret. Which means that: even when one knows about, learns of, the contents of a secret, what the secret contains, the secrecy of the secret—what is secret about the secret—perhaps remains secret from one; refusing to be secreted.

Which opens the possibility that when encountered with disappearance, with one who has disappeared, the questions— often the first ones that come to mind—*why can't I see her*, alongside, *where is (s)he to be found, to be seen again*, might well be the banal ones.

Where perhaps the better response, the more appropriate response—bearing in mind; and, this should be a burden on one, for it acknowledges the potential finality of this very disappearance—certainly the more interesting response, might be: *how to continue to hear her when (s)he is no longer here*.

How does one attend to her voice, continue to hear her voice, in not just the void, but in response to the void that is now her.

Where to be a fellow is to follow—not so much a course, certainly not a prescribed path, one that has been noted, annotated, charted, but to tune oneself to a call, to a voice, to a sound of thought, of thinking, that one thinks one hears, that is quite possibly only heard by one, can only be heard by the one who claims to follow, who names herself or himself as one who follows, who calls herself or himself a fellow.[xv]

To a rhythm, a cadence, quite possibly a song—to music that one might well have *made up*.

Perhaps with a dram, why not seven drams, of J&B Scotch— for, in this potential appropriation of JB, possibly imagined relationship with JB, somehow listening alongside, or even through, *whispers of whiskey* seems somewhat appropriate too.

ˣᵛ Quite unlike say Martin Heidegger, who refuses responsibility for responding to the call from the *Sturmabteilung*; dismissing his role, saying: « someone from the top command of the Storm Trooper University Bureau, SA section leader Baumann called me up. He demanded… »

Not a: I picked up the phone, answered the call.

But a: it wasn't my choice, not even really my doing—after all, « he demanded ».

Which translates to: *how could I not do so, how could I even say no.* Which is also an attempt at transposing genres: it is not so much a call but a *summons*: this was no ordinary sound made from a distance—he was a Storm Trooper, a figure from, and of, authority; it was daddy calling me… A strange response, particularly since it was coming from someone who had devoted his thinking to events, to possibilities, to the call of otherness.

For, why do some calls matter, and why do others not: and is it ever possible to dismiss a call that one has answered? Is it ever possible to constitute it as a call—or even a summons—if it was not answered?

But, as Avital Ronell reminds us in *The Telephone Book*, « if Heidegger was there to receive the SA call, it is because he first had to accept the Be-ruf, or position, from which that ordering call could be picked up, that of rector, a position he held from 1933 to 1934 ». Thus, this call « takes place within a context of a prior call, though not in terms of a subject's desire but in those of an inescapable calling or vocation ». If Heidegger could not turn down daddy's call, it was because he had first accepted the call, the *ruf*, to be a son. For, the very condition of its possibility as a call is that one answers, even if that answer is to turn away, to reject, to refuse the content of the call; the call itself is always already answered, at the very moment when one recognises that it is a call. And more

[29]

precisely—since one can never know if the call was even intended for one—by recognising its status as a call, one has already adopted it for oneself; and by doing so, opened oneself to its effects, to being affected by the call; by doing so, it is authorised as a call.

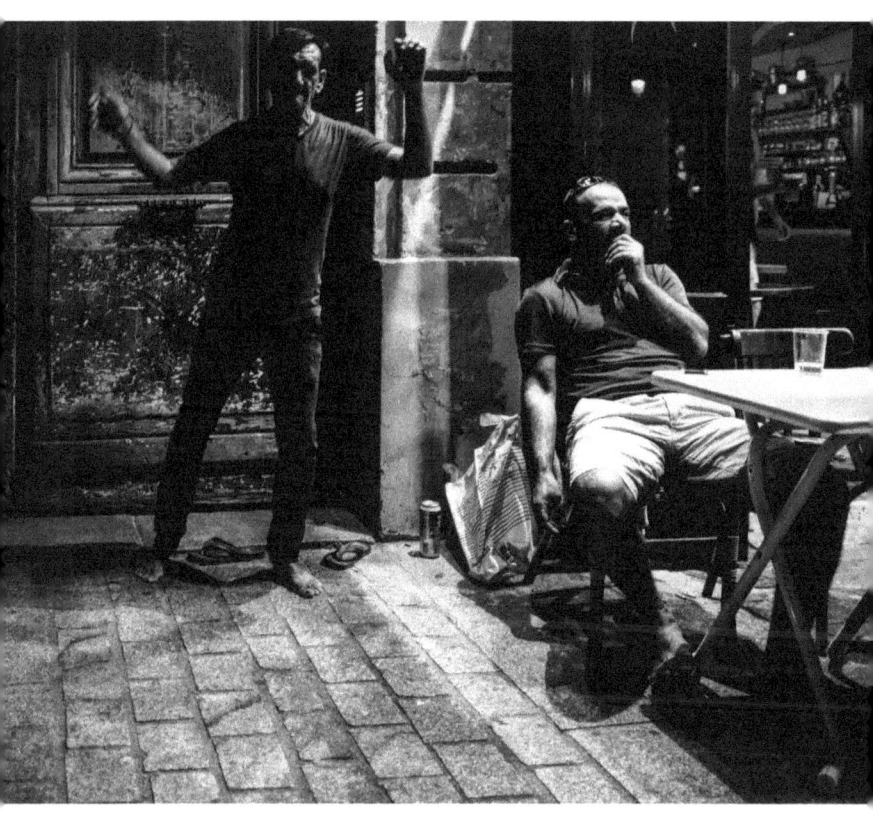

A FINAL, PARADOXICAL WINK...

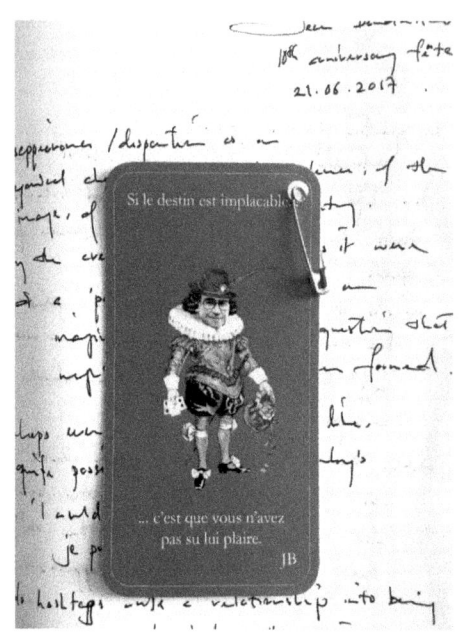

> …comes to us,
> perhaps came to us,
> is quite possibly always coming to us,
> from our dear friend, our teacher,
> to remind us, to quite possibly never let us forget, that
> the whole art is to know how to disappear before dying
> and instead of dying.

After all, he be the one who called for a disappearance even before he disappeared. Where, he was perhaps the one who had already disappeared even when he was with us; and now that he is gone, has played the final trick—has had the last laugh, as it were—not by returning, resurrecting, but by completely disappearing.

Leaving us not just with a memory, not just with his thoughts, his writings, but perhaps more importantly, his smile. For, as Marine Dupuis Baudrillard tells Wolfgang Schirmacher, « when I asked why he was smiling, he replied, what else can I do… ».

What else can I do…
…an utterance, his utterance, that comes—I would like to think—not through a want of volition, a lack of choice, but a *what else do I do but smile*. For, we should try not to forget that he had already—once upon a time—perhaps cheekily, warned us that nothing just vanishes; of everything that disappears there remains traces. The problem is what remains when everything has disappeared. It's a bit like Lewis Carroll's Cheshire Cat, whose grin still hovers in the air after the rest of him has vanished… Now, a cat's grin is already something terrifying, but the grin without the cat is something even more terrifying…

Which perhaps opens a question for us—a question that remains with us precisely by leaving, in its leaving, quite possibly in the moment in which it leaves—, the question of: *what is the art of disappearing?* For, if art is transformative, brings forth a new possibility, what is at stake is the ways in which disappearing has been changed, the manner in which our friend has altered disappearance. Or, if we want to be playful—and there is quite possibly no approach more appropriate during *une fête*—perhaps, what he has done is to have introduced us to the notion of appearances as a *diss*.

Where the art is in making a final, paradoxical wink—the wink of reality laughing at itself in its most hyperrealist form… irony. Where what remains—the grin—is nothing more, and infinitely nothing less, than a grin.

> Where, all one can say is: there is a grin.

> Even if it well might be
> —perhaps to our chagrin—
> his grin.

Which might be why Nietzsche reminds us that you should always *beware your disciples*. For they may, inevitably will, forsake you. Not through lack of faithfulness, certainly not for want of trying—but that in trying to interpret you, understand you, they will forget that in attempting to present you, they will always already be speaking over you, quite possibly be trying you, putting you on trial. For, in attempting to comprehend, they will always also be apprehending, stopping your movements, your vitality, perhaps your life itself—mortifying you, setting you into stone. Precisely because they will be trying too hard: for, in trying to preserve a tradition, preserve you as a tradition, what they will also be doing is delivering you, handing you over (*tradere*), and in doing so, be bringing forth the echo of, be ringing the bells of, treason (*trair*)—in trying to do this in memory of you, in attempting to keep you, hold on to you, all they will be doing is to be making you in their own image; that is, they will inevitably betray you.

Which is not to say that one ignores, doesn't attempt to attend to, the one whom one likes, admires, reads, learns from.

Far from it.

But, one should try to bear in mind that in order to touch, it is space that is first needed. Without which, not only is the other no longer wholly other, but that there is no longer any other.

Which might well be why another friend, one Sylvère Lotringer, reminds us to « forget meaning and with it the subject ». For, he continues, « beauty will be amnesiac or will not be at all ».

That it is only in the forgetting—of him, his work, even his thought—that we might be able to catch a glimpse of the beautiful. So, one might have to, quite literally, as the title of their conversation, the name of their interview, implies, perhaps even implores:

Forget Baudrillard.

After all, *a true friend stabs you in the front*.

For, this is the risk of having friends.

But perhaps, there is no love without betrayal, no infidelity that does not also bring with it echoes of, hopes of, a fidelity.

And this, this is the peril of friendship.
For, we have to bear in mind that *the risk of being a friend, of calling someone a friend, is that one of us will live to, will have to, watch the other die.*

A moment that I had to face one morning whilst lying in bed— that I am, in many ways, still facing.

3 in the morning.

On the 7th of March, 2007.

Tickets almost in hand to fly to Paris.

I receive a text message from a friend—a text bearing news which travelled from Paris to Leipzig, to Pretoria, finally landing in Singapore—a text from Tombie Rautenbach, carrying in it, with it, within it, a missive that read, that will always read,

« Baudrillard is dead ».

A text that continues to write itself onto me;
never forgetting that writing, what is written, quite possibly always also causes us to writhe.

> For, *words are missiles that explode in your somatic being.*

An explosion in me, into me, that has since been coming out of me.

Which is not to say that I know what it means, if it even means anything. In many ways, removing meaning brings out the essential point: namely, that the image is more important than what it speaks about—just as language is more than what it signifies… But it must also remain alien to itself in some way. Not reflect itself as a medium, not take itself for an image. It must remain a fiction, a fable…

Thus, so much more than painting a picture: where, by painting I also mean staining—adding a layer onto a medium, such that what is seen, what we call the painting, is what remains of the indistinguishable relationship between the canvas and the paint.

Where what we call a painting is what remains to wink at us— teasing us with the possibility that not only is it not what we think it is, say that it is, but, more radically, that, as Yves Klein might say, *the painting is only the witness who saw what happened.*

That, what we have named a painting quite possibility brings with it, bears, the secret name,
ceci n'est pas une peinture.

Much like writing.

Which is always an addition of something onto, a scratching into, a surface, but at the same time also what is scratched out of a material, from a medium. Where, what is read, what can be read, is perhaps what allows itself to be seen, to be glimpsed at—the remains of the skin which comes to us, the simulacrum, as it were.

So perhaps, all one can say of him is: he writes what he writes.
And all I can say of me is: *quod scripsi scripsi.*

This is writing so he can disappear;
writing his disappearance.

> Not just writing his radical alterity.
> But, writing as radical alterity.

And in writing on Jean, in writing his disappearance, what else can I do but smile…

Grin.
with a bottle of gin, no less…

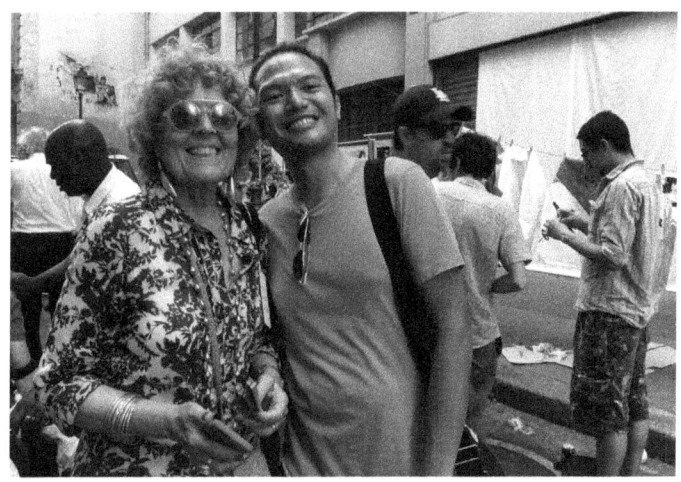

Marine Dupuis Baudrillard & Jeremy Fernando

All the lines, words, thoughts, in blue are echoes of and from Jean Baudrillard.

This piece was first delivered as a talk at the 10th anniversary *fête* celebrating Baudrillard's passing at the *Salon d'honneur in Le Conservatoire national des arts et métiers* at 2 Rue Conté.

With thanks, and much appreciation, to Marine Dupuis Baudrillard and Diane S. Rubenstein for the kind invitation, warmth, and hospitality; and to François L'Yvonnet and Marc Guillaume for organising the session.

UN ÉPILOGUE

par
Marine Dupuis Baudrillard

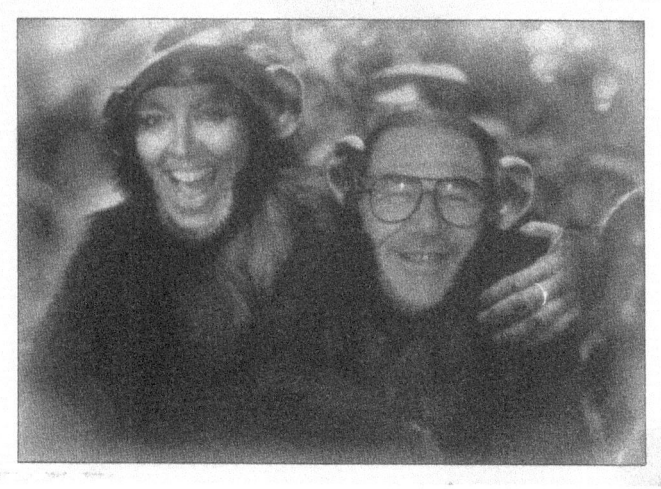

Image from Marine Dupuis Baudrillard

« Mourir n'est rien il faut savoir disparaître. Mourir relève du hasard biologique et ce n'est pas une affaire. Disparaître relève d'une plus haute nécessité. Il ne faut pas laisser à la biologie la maîtrise de sa disparition. Disparaître c'est passer dans un état énigmatique qui n'est ni la vie ni la mort ». ... mais pour moi Jean, cet état là ... qu'est ce que ça pouvait bien être d'autre que l'amour-toujours ?

Jean Jean Jean, Je te cherche et te trouve, toujours et partout ... dans les étreintes de ceux qui m'aiment (à ta place !) et dans les faux-fuyants de ceux qui m'évitent (à ta place !). Me donner ton nom ... fut le plus sûr moyen de m'aider à être autant qu'à disparaître ... une sorte de floutage ontologique ...

« Que l'illusion du monde te soit douce », m'as-tu souhaité en partant.

Depuis j'essaye d'être à la hauteur — ce qui est sans espoir bien sûr — mais ne me dissuade toujours pas de chercher à te plaire...

Et comme *« c'est le défi, c'est la séduction qui bien plus que le principe de plaisir nous entraînent au-delà du principe de réalité »* ... voilà comment, aujourd'hui comme hier, tu rends ta femme heureuse !

Marine
... et Jean Baudrillard

13 avril 2018
Paris

CONTRIBUTORS

Marine Dupuis Baudrillard met Jean in 1970 when she arrived at the University of Paris-Nanterre. She was 25 years old and was just back from a sailing trip around the world. Journalist (TV and magazines), artistic director, and scuba-diving instructor. They got married in 1994. She takes care of the *"Cool Memories" Association of Jean Baudrillard's friends.*
(contact@coolmemories.fr)

Jeremy Fernando reads, and writes; and is the Jean Baudrillard Fellow at The European Graduate School. He works in the intersections of literature, philosophy, and the media; and has written nineteen books, including *Reading Blindly*, *Living with Art*, *Writing Death*, and *in fidelity*. His writing has also been featured in magazines and journals such as *Arte al Límite*, *Berfrois*, *CTheory*, *Full Bleed*, *Qui Parle*, *TimeOut*, and *VICE*, amongst others; and has been translated into French, Italian, Japanese, Spanish, and Serbian. Exploring other media has led him to film, music, and the visual arts; and his work has been exhibited in Seoul, Vienna, Hong Kong, and Singapore. He is the general editor of the thematic magazine *One Imperative*, and a Fellow of Tembusu College at The National University of Singapore.

John WP Phillips teaches critical theory at The National University of Singapore. He writes about theatre, psychoanalysis, postmodernism, photography, philosophy, new media, music, military technology, literature, education, cities, and art. He has recently completed a book on Jacques Derrida and is currently writing a book on philosophy and its songs to the dawn.

Sarah and Schooling is a two-woman graphic design studio based in Singapore. An ardent supporter of Singapore's literary scene, the studio is actively involved in designing books and publications across multiple genres. Their capabilities and experience stretch beyond publications, reaching other creative disciplines such as visual identity and branding, art direction, web design, and conducting workshops.

www.ingramcontent.com/pod-product-compliance
Lightning Source LLC
Chambersburg PA
CBHW040522220526
45473CB00013B/2952